Printed in Great Britain
by Amazon

71482513R00072